MEL BAY'S *Clarinet* PRIMER

By Lou Hittler

Clarinet Primer is a beginner's guide to the clarinet. This text is especially useful for the trial or rental period. Great emphasis has been placed in this text on sound fundamentals, embouchure, and other basic techniques. Upon completion of *Clarinet Primer* the student will be ready to enter into Mel Bay's *Clarinet Method*.

1 2 3 4 5 6 7 8 9 0

CLARINET FINGERING CHART

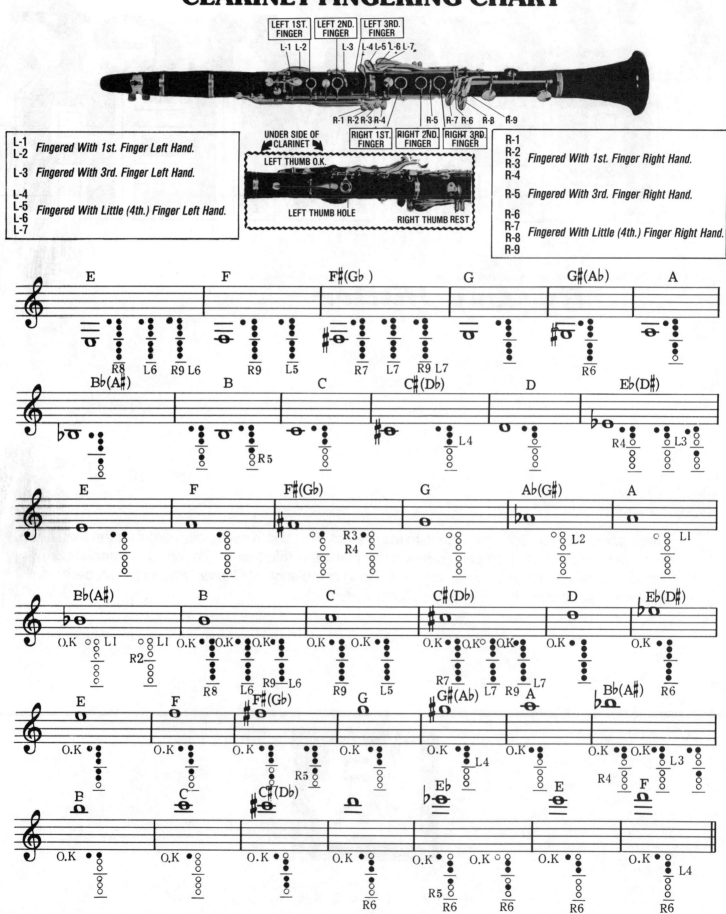

PARTS OF THE CLARINET

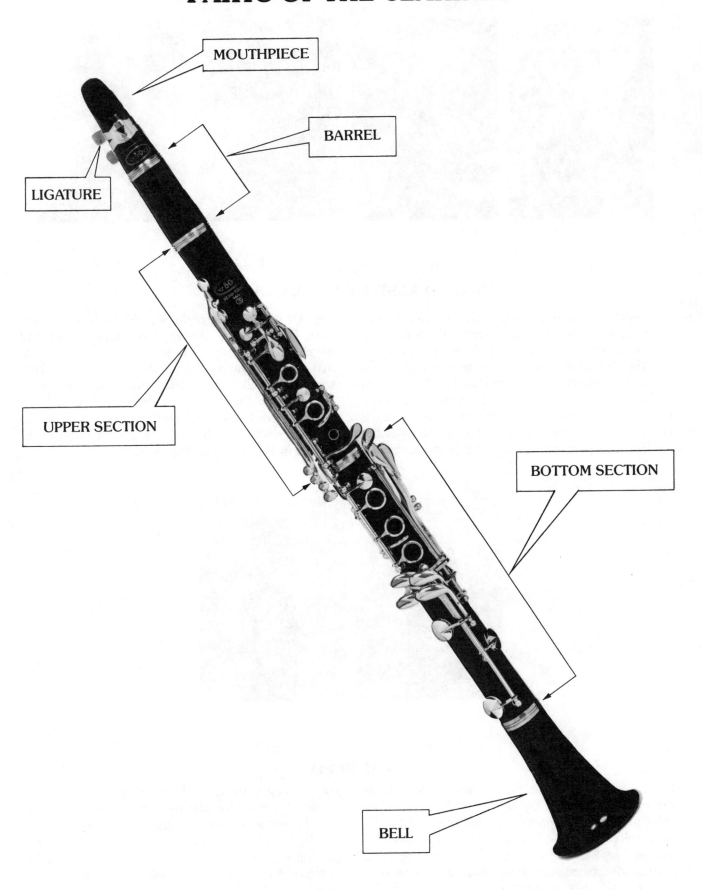

MOUTHPIECE

BARREL

LIGATURE

UPPER SECTION

BOTTOM SECTION

BELL

Fig. 1   *Fig. 2*   *Fig. 3*   *Fig. 4*

HOW TO ASSEMBLE THE CLARINET

We begin by putting together the two middle sections. Your left hand should depress the lower ring key, as shown in Figure 1. This is done in order to raise the bridge key. If the bridge key is not raised by pressing this lower ring key the clarinet will not fit properly together. The right hand should grasp the bottom section with the palm against the back of the instrument. Apply the pressure against the post or against the bottom padded key. Of course, the corks should be well greased with *Cork Grease*. Apply a gentle pressure and never force the clarinet together. Next, we add the bell section. The right hand should grasp the bottom of the bell and the left hand should be placed in a position similar to that shown in Figure 2. To connect the barrel and the mouthpiece onto the clarinet rest the bell on the knee for support as shown in Figure 3 and Figure 4.

Fig. 5   *Fig. 6*

THE REED

Place the reed on the mouthpiece as shown in Figure 5, so that the tip of the reed is even with the tip of the mouthpiece. Secure the reed to the mouthpiece with the ligature. Most teachers recommend a 2 or 2-1/2 reed for a beginner. It is a good idea to consult with your teacher to find out exactly what strength of reed he would like you to begin using. When not playing, always protect the reed by placing the mouthcap on the mouthpiece as shown in Figure 6. The instrument should be oiled periodically with a toothpick by putting key oil on the mechanism. Key oil may be purchased at your local music store. Be sure to use it sparingly.

Fig. 7   *Fig. 8*   *Fig. 9*

HOW TO HOLD THE CLARINET

Observe the above photos. First, place the right hand so that the right hand thumb rest sits on the first joint of the right hand thumb, Figure 7. Next, place your left hand in the proper position as shown in Figures 8 and 9. Do not hold the clarinet too tight.

Fig. 10   *Fig. 11*   *Fig. 12*

THE SITTING & STANDING POSITIONS

Notice the positioning of the elbows in Figure 10. They are not held rigid to the body, but are extended slightly away from the body in a relaxed manner. Your back should be straight when playing and the lower part of your back should touch the chair as shown in Figure 11. Do not, however, sit in a rigid position.

Notice in Figure 12 the position again of the elbows and the way the hands are placed on the clarinet.

5

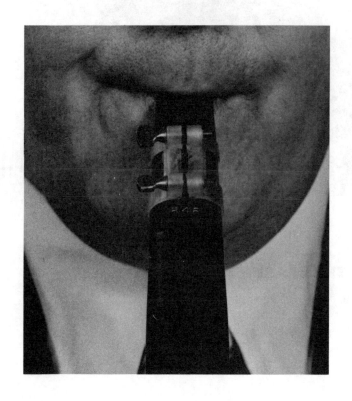

HOW TO GET A TONE
ON THE CLARINET

FRONT VIEW

The embouchure is the positioning of the lips around the mouthpiece. To form a correct embouchure, place your top teeth on the top of the mouthpiece about 3/8 of an inch from the top. Curl your bottom lip over your bottom teeth just slightly and bring the bottom lip up against the reed. The bottom lip should form a cushion as in whistling and the corners of the mouth should push in towards the mouthpiece. The top lip forms around the mouthpiece and keeps the air from escaping when blowing into the instrument.

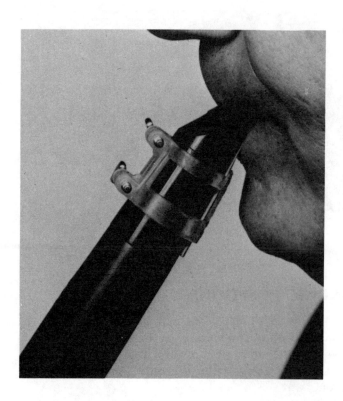

SIDE VIEW

The chin should not bunch up towards the reed, but it should remain flat and relaxed. The neck should be erect, but relaxed. Blowing will cause the reed to vibrate and this produces a tone. Start again with the tip of the tongue or just above it against the reed. Blow, release the tongue from the reed with a "doo" or "da" sound. This is called tonguing. Start all of the notes with this tonguing attack except where slurs or ties occur. Slurs and ties will be explained later on in the text.

OUR FIRST NOTES

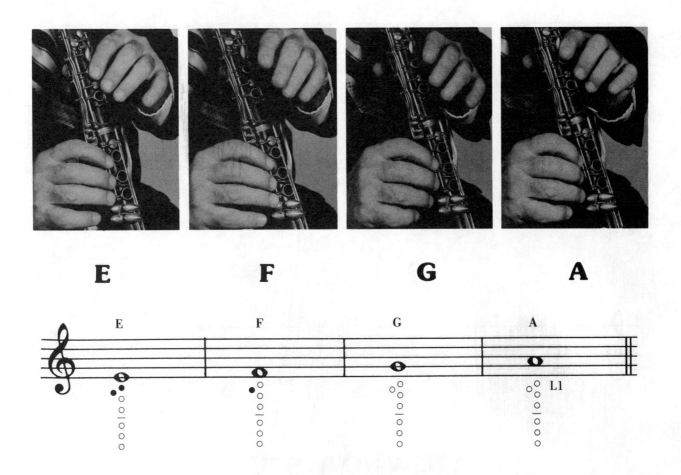

4/4 OR COMMON TIME

In $\frac{4}{4}$ time there are four beats to the*bar. Count "one and, two and, three and, four and." A whole note (o) gets four full counts. A whole rest (–) also receives four full counts.

*A Bar is the space between the vertical lines in music.

FIRST NOTES STUDY

MORE NOTES

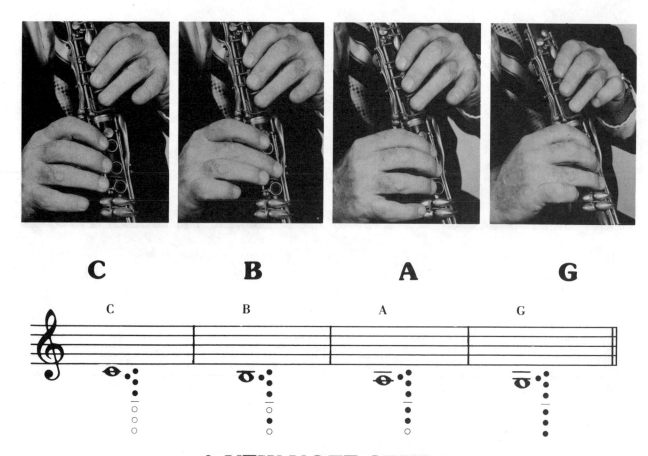

C   B   A   G

A NEW NOTE STUDY

ANOTHER
NEW NOTE D

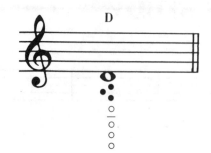

OUR FIRST SONG

Our first song is in $\frac{4}{4}$ time. A half note (♩) receives two counts. (One and, two and.) Observe all breath marks ('). Whenever these marks appear, you are to take a breath. Keep the breath flowing out smoothly and use the tongue to start each new note.

QUARTER NOTES (♩)

A quarter note receives one count (one and). Remember to use the tongue to start each new note. Do not start new notes by merely pushing more air through the horn.

ROW, ROW

GOLDEN SLIPPERS

SKIPS

THE TIE

A tie looks like this (⌒). A tie means that you tongue a note and hold (do not tongue) the note that the tie is connected to.

WHEN THE SAINTS GO MARCHING IN

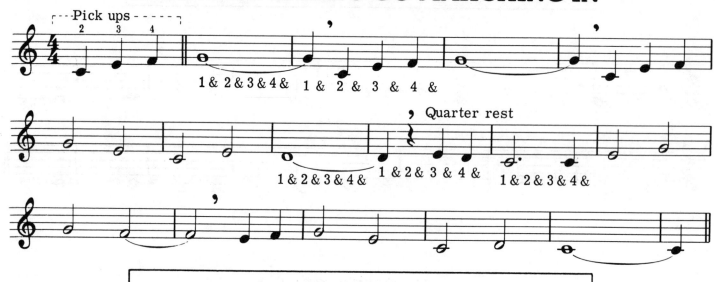

DOTTED HALF NOTE (𝅗𝅥.)

A dot after a note increases the value by one half of its former value. A dotted half note receives three counts. In this song, watch out for ties, dotted half notes, and a quarter note rest which receives one full count (one and).

AULD LANG SYNE

THE REST SONG

LONDON BRIDGE IS FALLING DOWN

TWINKLE, TWINKLE LITTLE STAR

"AU CLAIR DE LA LUNE"

A TISKIT, A TASKET

2/4 TIME

In 2/4 time, there are two beats to the measure. Count one and, two and.

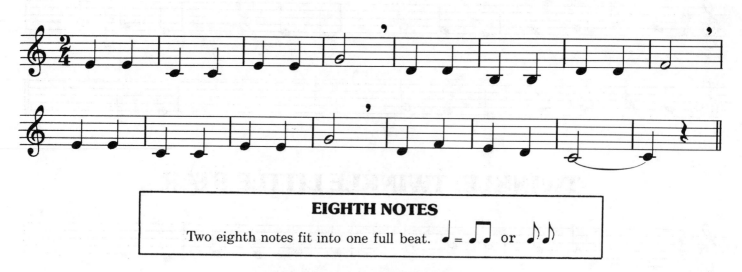

EIGHTH NOTES

Two eighth notes fit into one full beat. ♩ = ♫ or ♪♪

SKIP TO MY LOU

YANKEE DOODLE

JINGLE BELLS

A NEW NOTE B♭

B♭

ok   L1 - 1st. Finger
         Left Hand

THE FLAT (♭)

A flat will lower a note 1/2 tone. The flat is indicated at the beginning
of each song and will make all B's flat unless otherwise indicated.

THE SLUR

A slur is a long bracket that connects one or more notes. When a slur
appears, tongue only the first note and finger, but do not tongue all
of the following notes.

AURA LEE

One flat means we are in the key of F.

LOW B♭ & LOW F

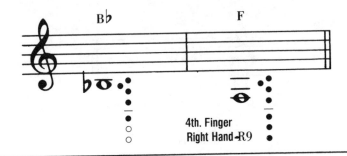

B♭   F

4th. Finger
Right Hand—R9

DOTTED QUARTER NOTE

A dotted quarter note looks like this (♩.). In the following song, we
have a dotted quarter. It receives one and one-half beats. Count "one
and two."

MARINES' HYMN

The same

Count: 1 & 2 &

14

3/4 TIME

In ¾ time, there are three beats to the measure, so we count "one and, two and, three and."

HOME ON THE RANGE

THE STACATTO

Stacatto means short and is indicated by a dot over or under the note. Tongue the notes short.

STACATTO SONG

– = *Hold full value.*

F# & LOW F#

THE SHARP

A sharp raises a note one-half tone. When a sharp, like F#, for example, is indicated at the beginning of a song this means that all F's throughout the song will be sharped, unless otherwise indicated.

BLUE BELLS OF SCOTLAND
One Sharp means we are in the key of G

MEXICAN SONG

16

STACATTO SCALE SONG

C# AND E♭

C#

4th Finger Left Hand — L4

E♭

R4

1st Finger
Right Hand

THE NATURAL SIGN (♮)

A natural is shown by the following sign (♮). This sign means to cancel out the sharp or a flat. In the following song, there is an F♯ in the key signature, so all F's should be sharped unless a natural sign occurs.

GOD OF OUR FATHERS

ACCIDENTAL SONG

DYNAMICS

At this point songs will be marked for volume. f means loud, mf medium loud, mp medium soft and p soft, pp very soft.
⟋ means get softer ⟍ means get louder.

ADESTE FIDELIS

The same

Ritard (means slow down gradually)

CAN CAN

SKIPPING SONG

Playing slurred skips is good for lip development. We will now play a song consisting of slurred skipping intervals.

MELODY

Fine (end)

D.C. al Fine

(means-go to beginning and play till *Fine* or end.

19

TWO KEYS IN ONE SONG

LONDON BRIDGE IS FALLING DOWN

ACCIDENTAL SONG

HIGH NOTES—D, E, F

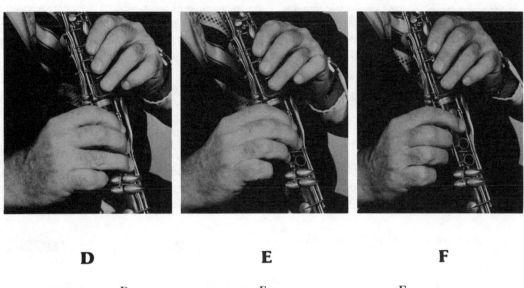

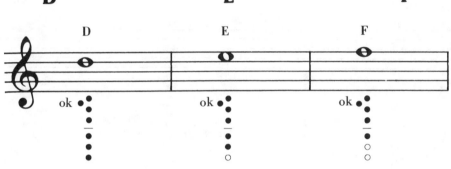

At this point, our lip muscle and finger technique should be developed enough to try some high notes. First, a few exercises and fingerings that will help. With these high notes, we use the upper register key. For convenience, we will call it an octave key.

A HIGH NOTE STUDY

21

MORE HIGH NOTES G, C, B, HIGH F#

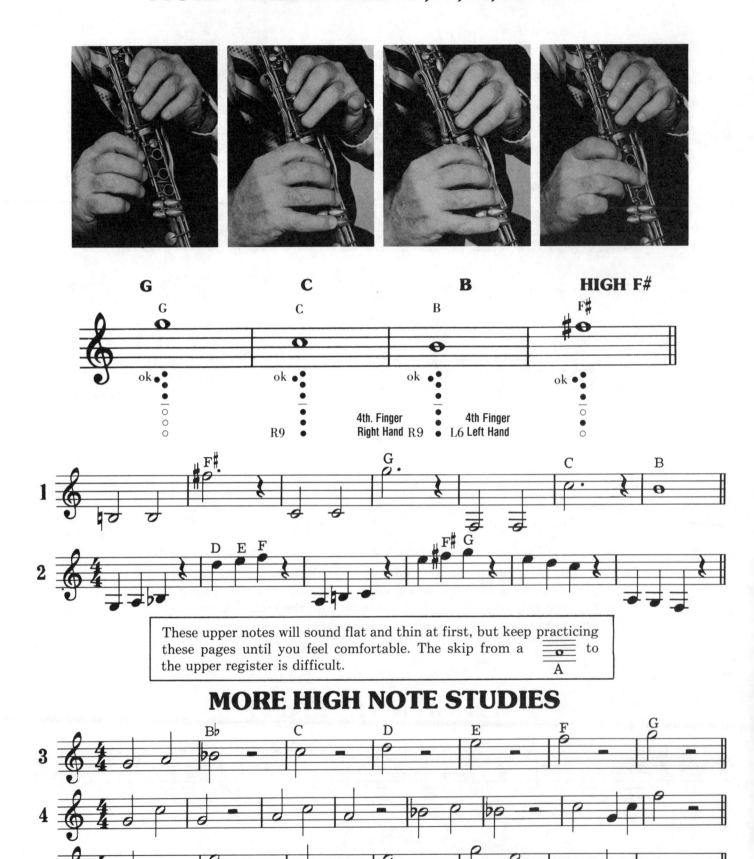

These upper notes will sound flat and thin at first, but keep practicing these pages until you feel comfortable. The skip from a ⊙ to the upper register is difficult.

A

MORE HIGH NOTE STUDIES

RED RIVER VALLEY

SHORT HIGH NOTE SONG

THE BLUES IN C

SWANEE RIVER

CAMPTOWN RACES
(IN TWO KEYS)